Essentials in Mechanical Drawing

ESSENTIALS IN
MECHANICAL DRAWING

THE MACMILLAN COMPANY
NEW YORK · BOSTON · CHICAGO · DALLAS
ATLANTA · SAN FRANCISCO

MACMILLAN & CO., LIMITED
LONDON · BOMBAY · CALCUTTA
MELBOURNE

THE MACMILLAN CO. OF CANADA, LTD.
TORONTO

ESSENTIALS

IN

MECHANICAL DRAWING

BY

L. J. SMITH, B.S.

PROFESSOR OF AGRICULTURAL ENGINEERING, MANITOBA AGRICULTURAL
COLLEGE ; FORMERLY INSTRUCTOR IN CHARGE OF THE DIVISION
OF FARM MECHANICS, MICHIGAN AGRICULTURAL
COLLEGE ; MEMBER OF THE AMERICAN
SOCIETY OF AGRICULTURAL
ENGINEERS

New York
THE MACMILLAN COMPANY
1917

Norwood Press
J. S. Cushing Co. — Berwick & Smith Co.
Norwood, Mass., U.S.A.

PREFACE

THIS brief treatment of the essentials of mechanical drawing is designed to give instruction in the rudiments of plan drawing as it occurs in everyday life, so that the student will be able to read and understand ordinary drawings and be able to do ordinary mechanical sketching. The book should be of value also to one who is about to take a longer course in drawing, for it aims to correct the common mistakes of the beginner.

Where work is given without the regular instruments, it is well to provide the students with small drawing boards about 12 × 18 inches in size, together with a T square. This equipment makes for more rapid and accurate work. The bottom edge of the drawing board can be planed square with the left side so that the T square may be used for both horizontal and vertical lines.

The lists of exercises offered are merely suggestive. Where possible it is best to have drawings made from the object itself rather than from another drawing. This is possible even in the drafting room, in institutions where shop work is given, for one can there secure enough joints or other woodwork so that at least every two students will have the object on the drafting table.

v

435850

Some of the drawings offer good exercises in making detail sketches of each piece in the object. Good practice can be had also in getting out the bill of material of the lumber required for some of the objects shown. The workbench or the pig cot furnishes the beginner a good exercise along this line.

While the book is designed primarily for use in the drafting room, the exercises shown are such as to be of value for use as a course in practical wood shop in schools of agriculture.

The writer believes that the time will soon come when our schools and colleges will consider elementary mechanical drawing at least equal in educational value to free-hand drawing.

L. J. SMITH.

MARCH, 1917.

ESSENTIALS IN
MECHANICAL DRAWING

ESSENTIALS IN MECHANICAL DRAWING

MECHANICAL SKETCHING

Introduction. — Mechanical drawing is, in these days of careful planning, the basis of all constructive work. The building of ships, the erection of the home, the large factory, or the sky-scraping office building, the construction of large locomotives, or of any of the great public works, is always preceded by very careful and complete drawings, previously planning all arrangements in detail.

A knowledge of mechanical drawing is not only essential in the constructive trades and professions, but it is of value in almost all walks of life. The newspapers and magazines make wide use of drawings. Educational books dealing with the more practical phases of life are illustrated in this way. Indeed, the general public will never get the benefit of many of the new ideas, nor be able to give others the benefit of their own experience, with-. out some knowledge and use of mechanical drawing.

It is not necessary to take a long course of instruction in order to be able to make or understand ordinary drawings. The making of six or eight pencil sketches will be sufficient to give the ordinary student a general knowledge of the subject. He will, of course, not become an expert, but he will have laid a good foundation for future development.

Neither is it necessary to have an expensive set of instruments in order to make sketches and learn to interpret drawings. With a good foot rule graduated into sixteenths of an inch, a compass fitted with hard lead, a fairly hard drawing pencil (3 or 4 H), and an eraser, it is possible with very little expense to make quite complicated drawings in lead, and to learn a great deal about lettering and drawing in general.

What mechanical drawing is. — In ordinary free-hand drawing where the work is done in " perspective," making picture drawings of the objects, the drawings usually show three sides of the object, or enough to completely represent it, in the one view. In mechanical drawing, the thing represented is shown by means of two or more views, each view showing one side of the object. In this kind of drawing, therefore, several views of the object are necessary and must be studied in relation to each other, in order to give a proper conception of that object. As an illustration, consider the object shown in Fig. 1, in one view only. In this drawing the eye sees three sides of the block at the same time and readily understands what is represented. A complicated drawing to accurate scale cannot readily be made showing three sides of the object, and so the idea of separate views has come into use.

Names of views. — Figure 2 shows a mechanical drawing of the same block, which is $2''$ [1] long, $\frac{3}{4}''$ wide, and $\frac{3}{8}''$ high on one side, and $\frac{3}{4}''$ high on the other. T represents the top view or plan of the block, S the side view or side elevation, and E the end view or end elevation. It will be noticed that the views are in line with each other,

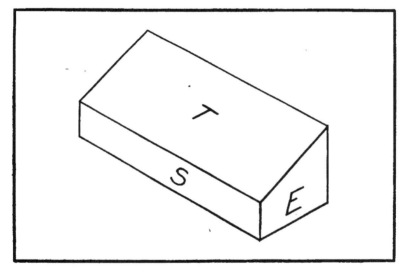

FIGURE 1.

that is, the top view is directly above the side view, and the end view is directly to the right of the side view, as shown by the light dotted lines which in practice are not drawn. The lines a and b will be parts of the same vertical line, and c and d of the same horizontal line.

[1] The two short dashes above at the right of a number denote inches, while one dash means feet.

The terms " plan " and " elevation " are used in connection with architectural drawings and many civil engineering drawings, while the word " view " is commonly
applied to other mechanical drawings. In plans for
buildings, the drawings of the various lay-outs of each
floor are called floor plans — first-floor plan, second-floor

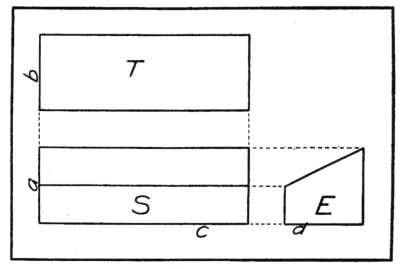

FIGURE 2.

plan, basement plan, etc. Sometimes the side, top, and
end views are not sufficient, in which case a drawing is
made showing part of the object cut away, and this
drawing is called a " sectional view." In reality the floor
plans of a building are sectional views, showing what
would be seen if the upper part of the building were cut
away down to the center of the windows of the particular
floor plan shown.

Position of the eye in relation to the views. — In mechanical drawing, if a top view is wanted, it is supposed to be drawn as seen by the eye placed directly above the object; if a side view is being made, the eye must view the object from that side; or if the end view is necessary, it is represented as if the eye were looking directly at the end of the object. The eye is supposed to be far enough away so that the rays of light coming from each point on the side of the object shown *enter the eye in parallel lines*. This must be continually kept in mind by beginners.

Isometric drawings. — The isometric drawing affords one of the most common methods of showing an object mechanically in one view only. In this type of drawing the object is drawn as viewed from such an angle that all edges of rectangular objects are cut down from their true length the same proportionate amount. Because of this fact the lines are commonly drawn *the same length as the lines of the object represented*. Figure 3 represents an isometric drawing of a half dovetail joint. The rectangular edges are usually drawn vertically, or 30 degrees from the horizontal (see Fig. 4); the vertical edges of the object being drawn vertical, and the edges running lengthwise and crosswise are drawn at an angle of 30 degrees from the horizontal. All other lines are obtained by reference to the lines representing rectangular edges.

The parallel lines of an object are shown parallel in isometric drawings instead of slightly converging as they do in perspective drawings. On account of this fact, isometric drawings of large objects do not look natural, and the use of these drawings is limited to smaller articles; but they are very serviceable in conveying ideas to those who are not able to understand mechanical drawings.

HALF DOVE TAIL JOINT.
Scale   Name.

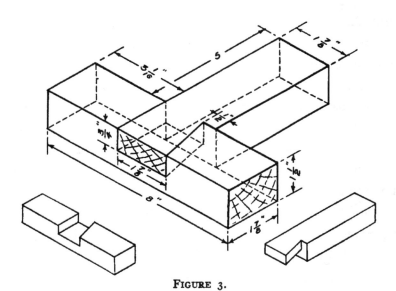

FIGURE 3.

To get the angle of 30 degrees where no 30 degree triangle is to be had, use the protractor; or in case none is at hand, draw an equilateral triangle with one side vertical to an imaginary horizontal line; the other two sides will be at an angle of 30 degrees with this line.

One can buy pads of 9″ × 12″ isometric section paper which is lined horizontally and vertically into squares,

and which has lines also running each way at an angle
of 30 degrees with the horizontal.

The angle iron in Fig. 4 is a very simple example of this

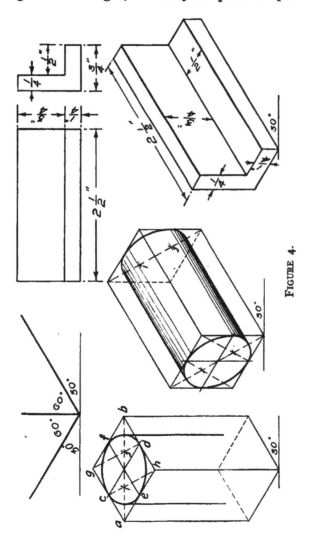

FIGURE 4.

type of drawing. It also gives the method of putting in dimensions.

Where the isometric drawings are made of cylindrical objects, the circle appears as an ellipse which is usually drawn by an approximate method. First draw an isometric square whose sides are the same length as the diameter of the circle. The ellipse will be drawn tangent to the center of the sides of the square at *c*, *e*, *d*, and *f*. Draw line *ab* and lines *cd* and *ef*. Draw *ch* and *gd*, and these lines intersect *ab* at *i* and *j* respectively. With these points *i* and *j* as centers, draw curves *ce* and *df*. Then with points *g* and *h* as centers, draw the curves *ed* and *fc*, completing the ellipse.

It is not difficult to make an isometric drawing of curved surfaces or edges. Figure 5 illustrates a common method of procedure. The end view and the end of the isometric drawing are divided into the same number of spaces. The lengths of the lines 1, 2, 3, etc., are measured on the end view of the mechanical drawing or the end of the object itself. Then the lengths are transferred to the ends of the isometric drawing, thus locating points on the curve.

Size of drawings. — Objects are represented on paper to different scales or sizes, depending on the size of the paper and of the object to be shown. Small objects are generally represented in the drawing in full or actual size. Very small objects may be magnified and shown on paper double their actual size. If the drawing is half size, the scale will be " 6 inches equals 1 foot," meaning that 6 inches of the drawing represents a foot of the actual object. The following are equivalent sizes and scales: —

Size	Scale
One half	$6'' = 1'$
One quarter	$3'' = 1'$
One eighth	$1\frac{1}{2}'' = 1'$ etc.

If a drawing is made full size, the scale is not put on the drawing, but simply the words " Scale, full size." In

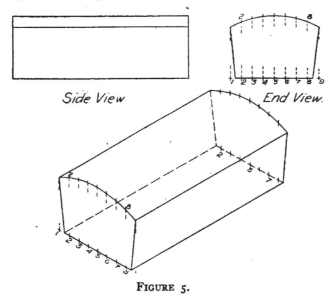

FIGURE 5.

architectural work and in other drawings representing large objects, the scale is very often as small as $\frac{1}{8}'' = 1'$. The ordinary rule with the inches divided into sixteenths answers very well for quite a wide variety of scales in mechanical sketching. If one is doing a good deal of this work, however, it is better to buy the regular triangular rule, which has twelve different scales on the one piece of wood. This rule, however, should never be used as a straight edge for drawing lines.

Dimensions. — No matter to what scale the drawing is made, *the full dimensions are put on the drawing*. This is very important. For example; if a drawing were made half size, and if the dimensions put on the drawing were also all reduced by half, then the drawing itself would be a full-size drawing of an object only one half as large as the one to be constructed; and, if so used, would result in the object being made half size.

As far as practicable, the dimensions are put at the bottom, and to the right of the various views: this, however, is not a fixed rule. Where there are a great many dimensions they are placed on all sides and often across the view itself when it does not confuse the drawing. In any case, the *dimensions should not be crowded too close to the lines which represent the various views*.

Figure 6 illustrates the proper method of putting in dimensions. A short dash and a longer one are put in, these being called " witness or projection lines." Then lines, called " dimension lines," are drawn *from the centers* of the longer dashes, and the dimension is put in at about the center, as shown. Arrows are drawn at the points where the dimension lines touch the witness lines. *The tip of the arrow should just touch the witness line*. In the case of the 2″ dimension shown in the illustration, the distance is indicated as being 2″ from the point of one arrow to the point of the other; and, as the witness lines are the same distance apart as the ends of the block, the dimension shows the block to be 2″ long. Often, as in the case of the ⅜″ dimension, there is not sufficient room between the witness lines for both the dimension and the dimension lines, in which case the dimension is put inside and the dimension lines and arrows outside the wit-

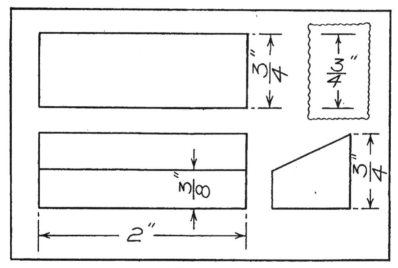

FIGURE 6.

ness lines; but the meaning is the same. It is ⅜″ from the tip of one arrow to the tip of the other, whether the arrows are on the inside or on the outside of the witness lines. In still another instance where there is very little room between the witness lines or between two lines whose distance apart is to be given, both dimension lines and arrows and the dimension may be put outside the two lines, as shown in the ⅛″ dimension, Fig. 7. The ¾″ dimension, shown in the upper right-hand corner of Fig. 6, shows a method of putting in a dimension very common with beginners, but one which is not considered the best practice.

How to make the arrows. — The arrows are not so easy to make as one might think. Properly made, they are at least twice as long as they are wide at the barbs, and are

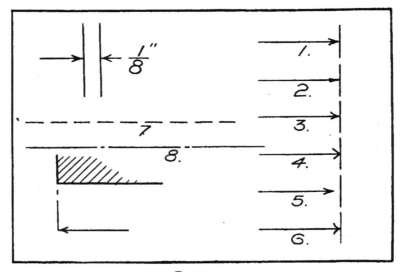

FIGURE 7.

made slightly curved, as shown by arrow 1, Fig. 7. Arrow 2 is in common use. It is made more easily, perhaps, but it is not so artistic and might lead to confusion where a number of witness lines or lines of the drawing are very close together. It has the objection also that it is likely to be the first thing that catches the eye at the first glance over a drawing, whereas the views should be first seen. Arrow 3 is not symmetrical about the dimension line. Arrows 4 and 6, shown in Fig. 7, illustrate incorrect shapes. Arrow 5 shows a very common mistake made by beginners in drawing, — that of not having the point of the arrow touch the witness line. Before starting a drawing make a dozen or more arrows, trying to make them as nearly as possible symmetrical with respect to the dimension lines. There is a tendency on the part of beginners to make the arrows too heavy on account of the fact that they cannot at first be put in by a single stroke of the pencil, but must be gone over several times in order to get the proper shape. In making arrows, therefore, make the strokes of the pencil very light, and avoid making the arrows too large and prominent.

Relation of border line to views. — When beginning a sketch of an object, first figure out the size of the views according to the scale to be adopted, and try to get the views in the center of the paper. It is customary to put in a border line which is first put in very lightly; then if the various views do not come quite in the center of the border line as desired, and if there is plenty of paper outside the border line for trimming, it can readily be shifted a little in any direction desired. The border line acts as a frame around the object shown, and for that reason should be made heavy, the heaviest weight line of any on the drawing. In some civil engineering drawings and in map work, two lines are often drawn and fancy corners are put in. Do not let any part of the drawing or the lettering touch the border line, and do not put printing outside the border line.

Penciling. — At first make the pencil lines of the drawing very light; then when the drawing is completed and one is sure that there are no mistakes, the lines can be gone over again and made heavier where they are not to be inked-in. This practice will save a good deal of erasing, and, therefore, will save time as well as assist in securing neatness, which is an important consideration in any kind of drawing. Heavier lines make a drawing stand out more clearly and give a much better appearance. The witness lines and dimension lines should always be put in much lighter than the lines of the drawing. When looking at a properly constructed drawing the first thing that the eye should see is the drawing itself, because

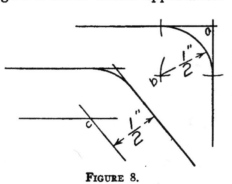

FIGURE 8.

of its greater weight of line; then, as a secondary consideration, the eye sees the witness and dimension lines and arrows.

Putting in curves. — When a corner in the view is to be rounded off, it is properly done by one of two methods. Suppose a right-angled corner is to be rounded with a curve of ¼″ radius. Set the compass to ¼″. Place the point at the corner *a* (Fig. 8), and strike off two arcs on the lines forming the corner. Then, with these intersections as centers, and with the same radius, strike off two arcs which meet at b, which locates the center for drawing the $\frac{1}{2}''$ curve. Where the lines do not form a right angle, the method of procedure is somewhat different. If, as in Fig. 8, a $\frac{1}{4}''$ radius is required, draw light lines parallel to and $\frac{1}{4}''$ from the lines on which the curve is to be drawn. The point c at which they meet is the center for the curve. This last method can be used with the right-angle corners.

When to use a solid or dotted line. — The following is a very good rule for the beginner to keep in mind when working on a mechanical drawing. Whenever two plane surfaces meet, forming an edge on the side of the object shown in the view, there is a solid line in that view. It makes no difference whether the surfaces meet at a right angle or at any other angle. If the two surfaces do not meet, making an edge, but rather round off with a considerable curve, then no line is shown except where one of the plane surfaces is parallel to the line of sight. Where two surfaces meet, but on the far side of the object so that the eye cannot see the intersection, the solid line is not drawn but a dotted line is used, as shown by line 7, Fig. 7. These rules are very important, and a careful observation of them will assist greatly in mechanical drawing.

How to make hidden lines. — In making these dotted lines, called " hidden lines " or " invisible lines," the dots, or rather dashes, must not be made too small nor too large. In ordinary drawings the dashes are made about one eighth of an inch long ; on large scale drawings a little longer, and on the small scale drawings they should be made shorter. In any case the dashes should be *all of the same length*. The spaces between the dashes should be *uniform* and should not be more than one half the length of the dashes. Hidden lines should not be made as heavy as the solid lines of the view.

Center lines. — When drawings are made of cylindrical or partly cylindrical objects, a center line is drawn in the side view through the center of the cylindrical part, and extends on through the end view of this part. Line 8, Fig. 7, shows the proper center line.

Breaking dimension lines. — If the dimension lines are very long, it is a common practice to break them up into two or even three long dashes, but this practice should not be carried too far. It is very seldom that more than two dashes should be put in as dimension lines on either side of the dimension.

Putting in large dimensions. — Where the dimension is greater than 36 inches, the length of the carpenter's rule, it is often not put down in inches, but in feet and inches. For example, 79 inches would be shown on the drawing as $6' - 7''$. A very common mistake is to leave out the dash between, thus $6'7''$. The objection to this practice is that the workman who might be making the object from the drawing is apt, in the hurry of the work and the possible worn condition of the much-used copy of the drawing, to make a mistake and make the object $67''$ instead of $79''$ long. The writer recalls seeing mistakes of this kind which usually proved expensive. When making drawings to be used by workmen, make it a practice to give every necessary dimension, for if it is necessary to add or subtract other dimensions to get what is wanted, there is always a chance of an error which might be costly.

The printing in of dimensions, explanatory notes, and the title constitutes the last, but by no means the least important, part of the drawing. Long after the beginner has acquired considerable facility in the making of good drawings, his lettering and figures will betray his inexperience.

Lettering. — There are four important things to be kept in mind when lettering. The first point is to have all the letters of a *uniform height*. In order to accomplish this readily, it is necessary to draw parallel lines to indicate the desired height of the letters or the figures. These lines should be drawn as lightly as possible, especially in case the drawing is not to be inked-in afterwards or traced for blue prints. By the use of the parallel lines the height of letters is sharply defined and there is no difficulty in getting uniformity in this regard.

The second item is that of making all the letters or figures of the *same slant*. In the system of lettering which is to be used (Fig. 9), the letters and figures are to be made with a slant of about 30 degrees from the vertical. It has been found that the slant system of lettering can be printed much faster than the old vertical system. On account of this fact, the tendency in modern mechanical drawing is to throw aside the old vertical system and more and more to

c

use the slant.   There is another reason for the use of the
slant system of lettering.   A little difference in the slant
of the letter or figure is not nearly so noticeable as a corre-
sponding difference where the vertical system is used.   The
eye seems naturally to be trained to notice anything that
is out of the vertical, but a slight variation in any given
slant is not so readily observed.

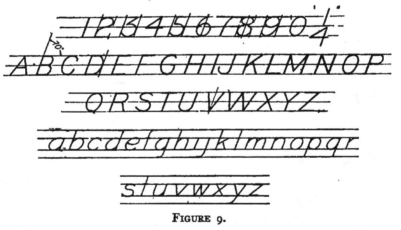

FIGURE 9.

Some difficulty is experienced by beginners in getting the
proper slant for such letters as X and Y.   The easiest
method of accomplishing this at the start is to draw a light
line at the proper slant, representing the center of the
letter, and then to make the letter symmetrical about this
line.

The third thing to be kept in mind in developing a good
system of lettering is the item of *spacing*.   This requires
considerable care at the start; but, after some experience
has been gained, letters and figures will be properly spaced

without much thought. The letters should not be put in at an equal distance apart, but the distance between the letters should be such that the *space or area between the letters is equal*. To illustrate, — the capital letters *L* and *M* must be as close together as possible where the *L* precedes the *M*, in order to get anything like uniform spacing. A glance at the sample lettering will show the necessity for carefully considering the spacing on account of the inequality in shape of the various letters and figures. In Fig. 9, the spacing between the capitals *F* and *G* is too great.

The fourth requirement is that the letters and figures should have *the same weight or thickness of line*. This is essential, not only in the more difficult work of inking-in letters and figures, but also in the pencil work. In ordinary lettering for mechanical drawings, no attempt is made to shade either letters or figures.

The main objects to be kept in mind in learning lettering for mechanical drawings are simplicity and speed as well as good appearance and clearness.

Figure 9 shows a system of lettering that is in very common use. Note the simplicity of the letters. There are no extra curves, only just enough to indicate the letters. This type of lettering is clear cut, can be read easily, and can be penciled in with speed when once mastered. As in any system of lettering, the exact shape of the letters must be memorized. To this end it is well to have at least one memory test in lettering the alphabet early in the drawing course in order to be sure that the proper shapes are being acquired right from the start.

For ordinary drawings, the capitals and the higher of the smaller letters are made $\frac{3}{16}''$ high, while the smaller letters are put in $\frac{1}{8}''$ high. The proper proportion is to make the body of the small letter three fifths the total height of the letter. For example, the body of the small letter b is three fifths of its total height. This, however, is a proportion which is rather hard to get, and the proportion of $\frac{1}{8}$ and $\frac{3}{16}$ works out very well and, if anything, gives a bolder and more rounding shape to the letter. The possible criticism to the letters and figures shown is that they are not broad and full enough. This is more apparent in connection with the capitals and the figures.

In putting in dimensions, the figures are ordinarily printed $\frac{1}{8}''$ high. If a fraction is used, each figure in the fraction is sometimes printed a little smaller, about $\frac{3}{32}$ of an inch in height, three quarters the height of the full number.

Good lettering *cannot* be done with a dull or very soft pencil. Sharpen the pencil to a long point and have a small piece of fine sandpaper at hand for keeping the point in good condition. It is of equal importance to keep the pencil sharp when making the drawings.

Titles. — The title of a drawing is variously located. The ordinary drafting office practice is to have the title at the lower right-hand corner. Figure 10 shows a simple form. The name and date are $\frac{3}{16}''$ from the lower border line. The lettering has $\frac{3}{16}''$ spaces between. The name of the object shown in the drawing is put in *capitals*, while in the case of the name, the scale, and the date, small letters are used. Often the title is located above the view or views as in case of Fig. 18 and Fig. 20; and sometimes it is placed in the center of the paper directly below the views as in Fig. 17. The important thing to be kept in mind when penciling in the title

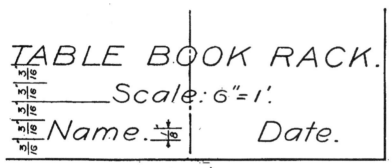

FIGURE 10.

is to make it *symmetrical*. If, as in Fig. 10, a center line were drawn vertically through the center of the name of the object, the line being equally distant from T and K, the other words in the title should be symmetrical about this center line. In the figure, the capital letter N in "Name" will be as far from the center line as the small letter e in "Date." No matter where the title is located, this practice should be followed.

SUGGESTIVE OUTLINE FOR A SHORT COURSE IN DRAWING, USING PENCIL AND RULER

Drawing periods. — There should be one drawing period a week if home work is given, or two periods without home work. Drawing periods should be one and a half to two hours, preferably two hours; each drawing to be done in one period, except the House Plans, which would require two or three periods. In case hour periods have to be used, two such periods would equal one of the longer ones. Definite instructions, by means of a rough sketch on the blackboard as to the location of the views in relation to the border line and a few of the main dimensions, will save much time. See Fig. 11.

Kind of paper to use. — If the drawings are to be done with a rule and pencil only, the edges of the paper used must form a rectangle with square corners, as the main outline of the drawing will have to be put in by measuring from the edges of the paper. A good quality of fairly heavy, smooth, white linen bond paper, $8\frac{1}{2}'' \times 11''$, is satisfactory for these exercises, or, better still, pads of the heavier white drawing paper of about the same size, or preferably a little larger, which can be had through the bookstores. The drawing can be done on any smooth table or desk;

sometimes it helps to have an extra sheet of paper underneath.

DRAWING EXERCISES

EXERCISE 1. — (Home work.)   Hand in a copy of the sample lettering in lead pencil, on a specified size sheet of

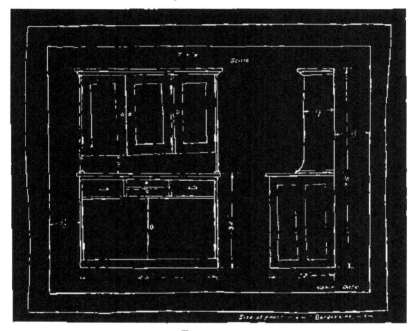

FIGURE 11.

paper, or on a small uniform size sheet given out for the purpose.   Make height of letters and figures the same as in Fig. 9.

EXERCISE 2. — Make a mechanical drawing of the half dovetail joint, using the dimensions in Fig. 3 and showing top and side views as in Fig. 12. Use the scale, 6″ = 1′. Put in all hidden lines. Put in a border line 1″ from the edge of the paper. Put title in lower right-hand corner, following the method shown in Fig. 10. Get the views in the center of the paper.

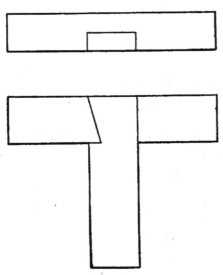

FIGURE 12.

EXERCISE 3. — (Home work.) Hand in an isometric drawing of the half dovetail joint. Scale, 6″ = 1′. Put in all dimensions, but do not put in a border line or show hidden lines. Title and its location as in Exercise 2.

EXERCISE 4. — Make a half size isometric drawing of the mortise and tenon joint from Fig. 13, border 1″ from the edges of the paper, title at the top as in Fig. 3. Draw all hidden lines, but not the parts of the joint separately.

EXERCISE 5. — (Home work.) Hand in an isometric drawing of a bench hook (Fig. 14). Do not use a border line. Put title in lower right-hand corner. This bench hook is made from one piece of wood. Read over the notes on isometric drawing, beginning on page 5.

EXERCISE 6. — Make a mechanical drawing of the blacking stand shown in Fig. 15. Scale, 3″ = 1′. Border line, 7″ × 10″. Draw the views ¾″ from the side border lines. The body of the box is 16″ long and 11″ wide. Make the stand a convenient height for use. Work out all dimensions. On a separate sheet of paper hand in a

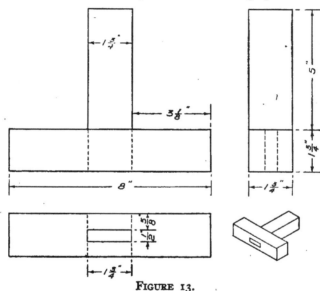

FIGURE 13.

bill of the material required to make the blacking stand, using the form given below. The pieces must be of dimen-

NAME OF OBJECT

*Kind of material*_____   *To be finished with*_____

No. of Pieces	Thickness	Width	Length

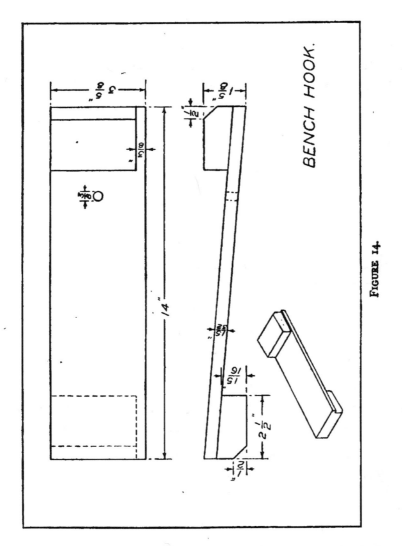

BENCH HOOK.

FIGURE 14.

sions large enough to allow for finishing to required size in the wood shop. For example, a 12″ board would be used for the vertical end pieces; in actual practice the board will be about 11¾" wide.   Timber is sold as 6", 8", 10", 12", 14", etc., wide, but when actually measured it usually is ¼" less.   A 1" finished board is actually about 1⅜" .thick.   In the rough it is about 1" thick.   An ordinary 2"

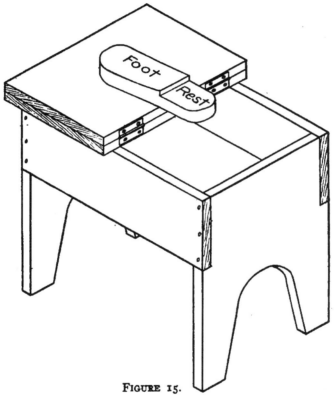

FIGURE 15.

× 4" finished on all sides (S2S) is actually about 1⅝" × 3⅝"; the 2" × 6" is 1⅝ × 5⅝". These points must be kept in mind when planning the dimensions of wooden objects in order to economize in material. Many good draftsmen neglect this important matter.

EXERCISE 7. — (Home work.) Hand in a mechanical drawing of the wooden work basket, a suggestive outline of which is shown in Fig. 16.   It is 26″ high and 14″ square. Scale, 3″ = 1′.   No border line.   Material, oak.   Draw a side and a top view.   Put title in lower right-hand corner.

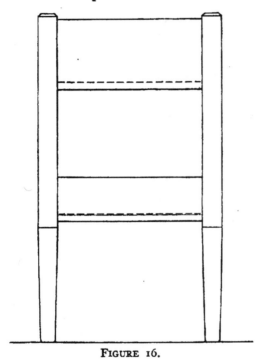

FIGURE 16.

EXERCISE 8. — Make a mechanical drawing of a poultry feed hopper (Fig. 17). Scale, 3″ = 1.′ Use no border line. In this case there is not sufficient room ⸱ on the 8½ × 11″ paper ⸱ to show the entire side view; ⸱ part of the middle is, there-fore, taken out, as shown by the broken lines. This is often done in drawings of long objects of uni-form size and shape. As the slanting board cannot be seen, except by hidden lines, in an end view, a sectional view is shown as if the box were cut away at A — B. Put in title as in Fig. 17.

EXERCISE 9. — (Home work.) Hand in a mechanical drawing of the table bookrack (Fig. 18) on cross-section

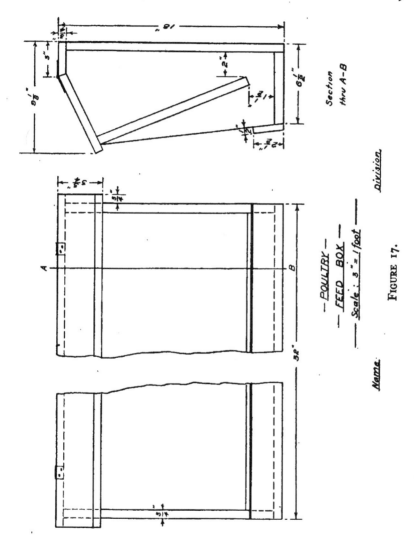

FIGURE 17.

paper. If the squares are 16 to the inch, let 4 squares
equal 1 inch. If the paper has 8 or 10 squares to the inch,
let 2 squares equal one inch of the object.

Cross-section paper is very useful for the rough sketching of objects, and particularly for making preliminary plans of barns or houses. Let agricultural students, instead of drawing the table bookrack, make a drawing of the gambrel

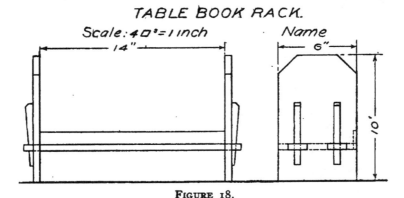

TABLE BOOK RACK.
Scale: 4□°= 1 inch   Name

FIGURE 18.

roof with bracing, as shown in Fig. 19. Draw foundation 1 foot thick. Scale, $\frac{1}{4}'' = 1'$. Put the following title below the drawing : —

METHOD OF BRACING GAMBREL ROOF

SCALE

*Name*_____   *Date*_____

The figure gives a fairly good idea of one method of framing the gambrel roof. It also gives a good proportion for such a roof, the rafters being equal in length, and the cuts easy to work out. The sketch is for a 36' barn. The studding, rafters, and braces forming the bent are all 2 × 6's. There are two kinds of framing, one on each side of the center line. The bent shown on the left side is put in every fifth or sixth rafter, and of course is the same on both sides of the peak, only one half being shown in the cut.   The sets of rafters between these bents are tied together as shown on the right side, with $1'' \times 6''$ stuff.   The hay track

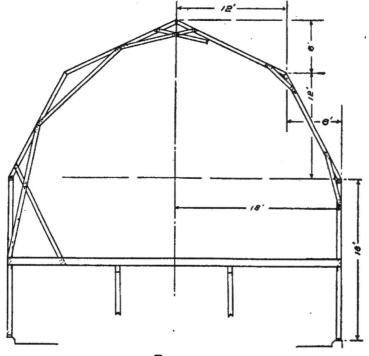

FIGURE 19.

can be hung from the intersection of the scissors truss, if desired, or a $2'' \times 6''$ collar tie can be used at the same level as the intersection just mentioned,   The lower $2'' \times 6''$ brace, that projects out into the loft at the bottom, is not always used, as it cuts up the loft to a certain extent.   It would not necessarily have to extend out as far as shown.

In wide barns the brace should not be left out. Often two studs are used at each bent, and it is a good practice when building barns much over 30 feet in width and height.

EXERCISE 10. — (For boys.) Make a copy of the plan of a barn shown in Fig. 20. Scale, $\frac{1}{8}'' = 1'$. Make the outside walls 1 foot thick. Put title in center above the plan.

Figure 20 shows an excellent type of dairy barn. It is the plan of the model dairy barns used on the Alberta Experimental Farms located in different parts of the Province. The plan shows a central feed room in the most convenient relation to the feed alleys. The grain bins are overhead in the loft. The plan can be readily extended or rearranged. If one wanted an inclined driveway into the loft, it could easily be arranged just outside the bull pen, or at the opposite end of the feed passage. A root cellar could then be put under the incline. It could be extended to the left enough to take in the feed passage, thus affording a convenient entrance to the root cellar. If desired, a concrete milk room could be put under the driveway. The cross feed passage at the end makes it very easy to put on an additional wing at either side, making an L-shaped barn, with the added space available either for more cow stalls, or for a horse barn, if so desired. Again, a root cellar might be placed at one end of the cross passage, and a silo at the other; the silo being placed on the sunny side of the barn. The farmer might cut down the width a little, if

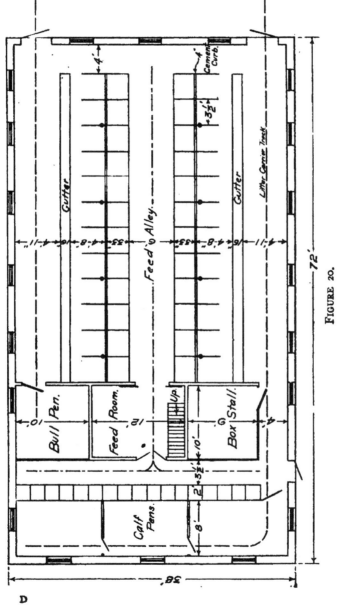

FIGURE 20.

he so desired, by economizing in the width of the feed passages. The barn has the gambrel roof that is being used so widely in modern barn construction.

(For girls.)   Copy two plans of the model kitchens in Fig. 21.   Scale, $\frac{1}{4}'' = 1'$.   Put title "MODEL KITCHENS," etc., in lower right-hand corner.

The kitchen is said by many women to be the first consideration in house planning, since it is the part of the house where they do a large part of their work and where there is the greatest necessity for convenience and comfort.   It should, therefore, be carefully thought out, and there should be no great difficulty in securing a house plan that the kitchen will fit into.   If the house is planned without particular thought about the requirements of the kitchen, it often develops that the rest of the house will not admit of a convenient kitchen lay-out.

The suggestive plans in Fig. 21 are from well-known women writers on household science.   Plan 1 is from the *Efficient Kitchen* by Georgie Boynton Child.   Plan 2 is from *The Farm Kitchen as a Workshop*, U. S. Farmers' Bulletin No. 607, by Anne Barrows.   Plan 3 is from Mrs. Fredrick's book *The New Housekeeping*.   This is an especially suggestive plan, as it shows by arrows the cycle of operations in the preparing of food for the table, and the washing and putting away of the dishes after the meal is finished.   The kitchen in the plan shown in Fig. 22 is one which allows for good light and air as well as for convenience. Make the kitchens whatever size you consider best for your

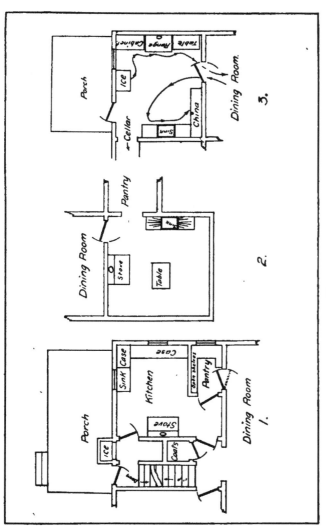

FIGURE 21.

home conditions. The dimensions of kitchen furnishings on page 38 will be of assistance.

EXERCISE 11. — (Home work.) Hand in a mechanical drawing showing side and end views of a table, bookcase, or dresser. Scale, $1\frac{1}{2}'' = 1'$. If there is room, put in a border line. Draw a line representing the floor on which the object rests. Put title below the view.

EXERCISE 12. — Copy the floor plan of bungalow shown in Fig. 22, or some other plan of a bungalow or house. Use the scale, $\frac{1}{4}'' = 1'$.

In drawing floor plans of a wooden house, make the walls 6'' thick — both outside and partition walls. Single windows are 28'' to 30'' wide; large front windows are $3\frac{1}{2}'$ to 4' wide. The front door is usually 36'' wide; the outside kitchen door 30''; the double swinging door between the kitchen 28'' to 30''; doors to bedroom closets 24''; door to bathroom 26'' to 28'', and other doors 28''. These are average sizes, though there is considerable variation.

Stairs vary widely in dimensions. Where there is room, a very good stair is one with a 7'' rise, and a 10'' tread. A $7\frac{1}{2}''$ rise and a $9\frac{1}{2}''$ tread gives an easy running stair. Cellar and attic stairs are steeper, in many cases the rise and tread being equal, as $8\frac{1}{2}''$ for both rise and tread.

In house planning, doors are usually located in the corner of the room. Doors and windows in bedrooms should be so located as to avoid drafts across the bed.

Sizes of furnishings. — The following is a list of common furnishings, together with their average dimensions, and

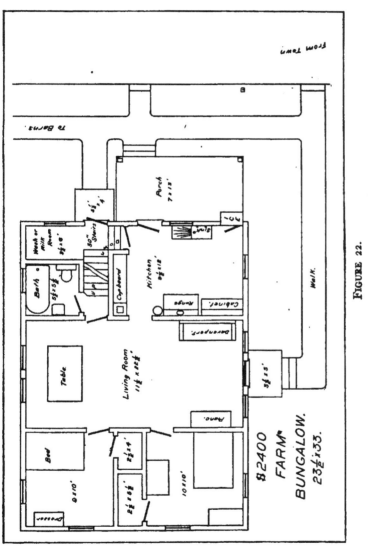

FIGURE 22.

is useful for consideration in planning the sizes of rooms
and location of doors and windows: —

Double Bed	4 to $4\frac{1}{2} \times 6$ feet
Single Bed	3 to $3\frac{1}{2} \times 6$ feet
Child's Bed	$2\frac{1}{2} \times 4\frac{1}{2}$ feet
Dresser	$1\frac{2}{3} \times 3\frac{1}{2}$ feet
Dining Room Table	$3\frac{1}{2} \times 6$ feet
Living Room Table	$2\frac{1}{2} \times 3\frac{1}{2}$ feet
Bookcase	$1\frac{1}{4} \times 3\frac{1}{2}$ feet
Piano	$2\frac{1}{2} \times 5$ feet
Davenport	$2\frac{1}{2} \times 6$ to 7 feet
Bathtub	$2\frac{1}{2} \times 5$ feet
Range	$2\frac{1}{2} \times 4$ feet
Kitchen Cabinet	2×4 feet
Kitchen Sink	$1\frac{1}{2} \times 2$ feet
Drain Boards to Sink	$1\frac{1}{2} \times 2$ feet
Refrigerator	$1\frac{2}{3}$ to 2 $\times 2\frac{1}{2}$ feet

MECHANICAL DRAWING WITH REGULAR. DRAWING EQUIPMENT

Equipment. — For this work, the following equipment is necessary: drawing board 18″ × 24″, a T square, a 30°–60° triangle, a 45° triangle, a draftsman's triangular

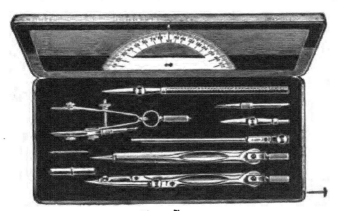

FIGURE 23.

scale, some thumb tacks, a bottle of Higgins' black ink, a set of drawing instruments, and a pencil and eraser. A small set of drawing instruments that will do very well can be purchased for about $3. Figure 23 shows such a set of instruments which consists of a ruling pen, a small combination bow compass and pencil, a pair of bow dividers, a large compass with a pen and a pencil point and an extension bar for large circles, and a protractor. The rest of the drawing equipment will cost about $3 more. To avoid confusion, it is highly desirable that the students should put their initials on their equipment.

The left edge of the drawing board must be true, for the head of the T square slides against this edge. Drawing boards, when first purchased, generally need " truing-up " on the edge with a jointer plane. The T square, sliding against the edge, is used for making all horizontal lines, while the triangles, resting against the blade of the T square, are used for making all vertical lines. Draw horizontal

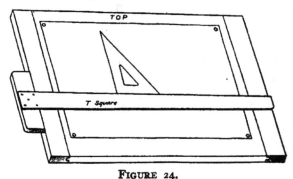

TOP

T Square

FIGURE 24.

lines with the pencil against *the upper edge* of the blade of the T square. Figure 24 shows the drawing board with T square, 30°–60° triangle, and drawing paper, ready to begin work.

Steps in penciling and inking drawings. — 1. Put drawing paper on center of board, fastening with four thumb tacks, and having horizontal edges parallel to blade of T square.

2. Draw border line *lightly* to required size.

3. Lay out position of views, keeping in mind position of title.

4. Draw main lines of views.

5. Draw hidden or invisible lines.

6. Put in witness and dimension lines.

7. Put in dimensions and arrowheads.

8. Print in title, and notes if any.

9. Ink-in border line *heavy*.

10. Ink-in curves.

11. Ink-in views.

12. Ink-in witness and dimension lines.

13. Ink-in dimensions and arrows.

14. Ink-in title and notes.

Inking-in drawings. — The best ink for this purpose is Higgins' Carbon Waterproof Ink. There is also Higgins' Black Ink which is not waterproof. The latter is just as good except for the reason that sometimes one may be carrying a drawing on the board exposed to the air, and a few flakes of snow, or drops of rain, may fall on it, in which case the ink which is not waterproof softens and, if rubbed in that condition, will spread and spoil the drawing.

Always keep the stopper in the bottle, as it keeps out the dust and prevents accidents if the bottle is tipped over. When filling the pen by the·use of the stopper, do not perform the operation above the drawing, as there is always danger of dropping some ink; nor should one fill the pen too full nor allow it to get entirely empty.

The first care in inking-in drawings is that the surface be free from dust, particles of eraser, lint, etc. Any such material is caught up by the pen and will change the thickness of the line. Next, and equal in importance, is the care of the inking pen, whether it be for the compass or for the straight line work. The pen must always be free from ink, either wet or dry, on the outside surfaces of the two points, and from dry ink on the inside surfaces. Under no circumstance should ink be allowed to dry in the pen. The piece of linen which comes around the ink bottle is for cleaning the pen, but any cloth free from lint will do. ˙

Before starting to ink the first drawing, examine the points of the pen; they should be sharp and of *equal length*. In case they are not, make them equal by rubbing them on an oilstone. To tell whether they are in good shape, screw the points almost together and hold them up to the light. When inking, tip the handle of the pen about thirty degrees from the vertical (Fig. 25) in the direction in which the line is to be drawn, but keep the pen in the vertical plane which passes through the line so that both points of the pen rest with equal pressure on the drawing paper. If one point touches and the other does not, the line drawn will be ragged and rough on the side where the point of the pen does not touch. Careful attention to this principle will greatly improve the work of beginners.

Use of compass. — When inking with the compass observe the rules just given. Hold the compass *lightly* at the extreme end between the thumb and first or second finger and make the circular motion by rolling the end of the compass between the surfaces of the thumb and finger. Do not press down hard. When there are curves to be inked-in on a drawing, always ink them *first*. It is far easier to ink-in a straight line to meet one end of an inked curve, than to ink-in a curve to meet two straight lines.

Inking on transparent linen tracing cloth is a little more difficult operation than working on paper. The glazed

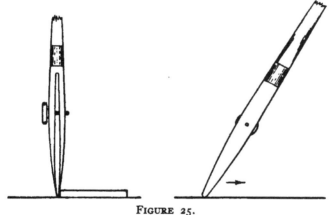

FIGURE 25.

surface does not take the ink so readily and the ink does not dry so quickly. Many consider it preferable to ink on the glazed side, as there is more starch on that surface, which permits erasing. Before starting to ink, rub an ordinary blackboard eraser over the glazed surface so that it will take the ink more readily. Be careful to wipe off the chalk before beginning to ink. The majority of draftsmen prefer to use the dull side, as it takes the ink better.

SUGGESTIVE LIST OF EXERCISES FOR A SHORT COURSE IN DRAWING WITH INSTRUMENTS

This course will require twenty two-hour drawing periods, one period a week. It is well to set a definite time for each exercise to be finished, in order that those a little behind may catch up with the rest. All exercises to be inked-in.

EXERCISE 1. — Hand in a copy of the sample lettering on a piece of drawing paper 6″ × 8″, with a border line 4″ × 6″. Make letters same height as in the copy. Print name at lower right-hand corner inside the border line. Use light pencil lines to guide when lettering, and erase them after the ink is dry. This exercise is to be done outside of the regular drafting periods.

EXERCISE 2. — After laying out Fig. 26 very carefully with a *sharp* lead pencil, start inking it. The large square is 5″ each way and is divided into 2½″ squares. The lines are all spaced ¼″ apart at the edge of the squares. To get good results, the laying out of the squares and the spacing must be done very accurately. The beginner may spoil the first drawing, but that is to be expected. Finish the first drawing as carefully as possible, even if some parts are not satisfactory, as the exercise is for the purpose of giving experience in the use of the pens. This experience gained on a small drawing will prevent one's spoiling a more complicated drawing later on.

After the first set of squares has been filled in carefully, make a second drawing of the squares. The beginner should now have sufficient experience from the first trial to do some good inking on the second drawing. When

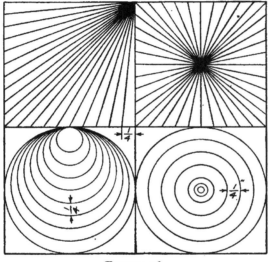

FIGURE 26.

inking-in the lines that converge to the upper right-hand corner in the upper left-hand square, ink the lines to within about $\frac{1}{8}''$ of the corner; then when all the lines have been inked-in, the part not done can be completed. By following this method the point at the upper right-hand corner will not be lost, and the work can be more accurately done. Ink-in the outside of the squares after all the other work is completed. Hand in this exercise on a sheet 6″ × 8″ without a border line and with name neatly printed in ink in lower right-hand corner.

EXERCISE 3. — Make a full-size drawing of the wooden float in Fig. 27. Size of border line 11″ × 15″. Trim the

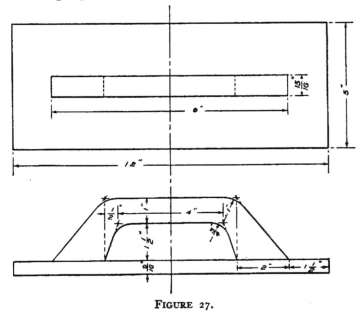

FIGURE 27.

drawing paper to within ⅛″ of the border line. Put title at top.

EXERCISE 4. — Mechanical drawing of blacking stand (Fig. 15). Show side view of stand open and end view. Follow the general directions given in Exercise 6 on page 24. Use a border line 11″ × 15″. Print out table of material underneath the views.

EXERCISE 5. — Make an isometric drawing of the bench hook shown in Fig. 14, scale full size. Ink hidden lines

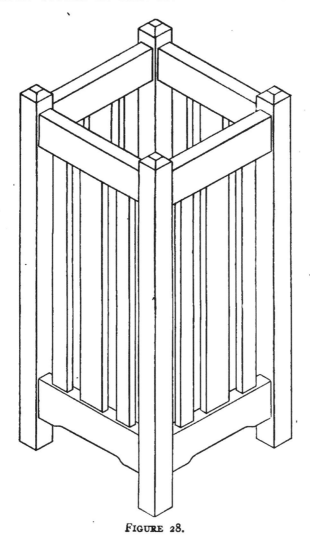

FIGURE 28.

considerably lighter than the solid lines.   Put title in lower
right-hand   corner.   Border   line   11″ × 15″.   Trim   all
drawings to within ¼″ of the border line.

EXERCISE 6. — Drawing of work basket (Fig. 16) or umbrella stand (Fig. 28). The work basket is to be 14″ square and 26″ high. The umbrella stand is 12″ × 27″.

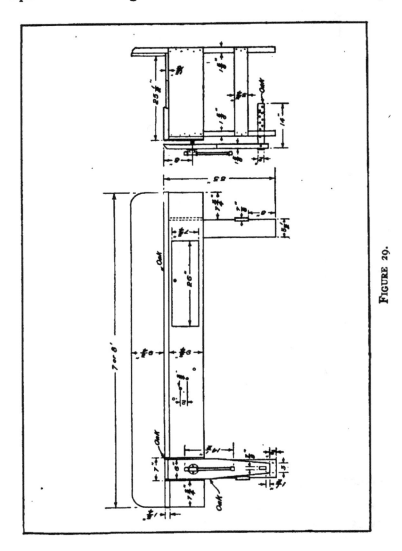

FIGURE 29.

Use the scale, $3'' = 1'$ in either case, and the standard border line $11'' \times 15''$. Show a side view, and top view to the right of the side view. If the student has had wood · shop, show the mortise and tenon joints. Show all dimen-

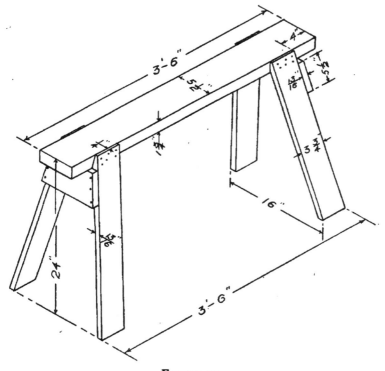

FIGURE 30.

sions. Underneath the top view, print the bill of material as already directed.

EXERCISE 7. — Make a side and end view of either a work-bench (Fig. 29) or a sawhorse (Fig. 30). The workbench to be drawn to a scale of $1'' = 1'$. Often, when objects are

E

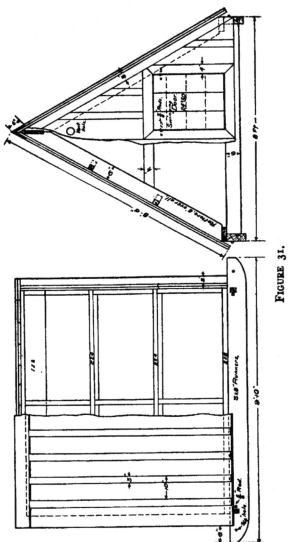

FIGURE 31.

drawn that naturally rest on the floor, a heavy line is drawn to represent the surface of the floor. Border line $11'' \times 15''$. Place title above the views. The sawhorse should be drawn to the scale, $3'' = 1'$. Draw a heavy line to represent the floor.

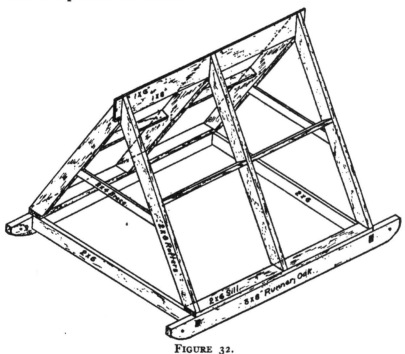

FIGURE 32.

EXERCISE 8. — Draw side and end views of a portable pig cot (Fig. 31) with part of the roof boards and siding cut away to show the framing. Scale, $\frac{3}{4}'' = 1'$. Use the $11'' \times 15''$ border line. Place the title above the views. Figure 32 shows the framework of the pig cot. First draw the end view of the frame of the pig cot. The rafters are

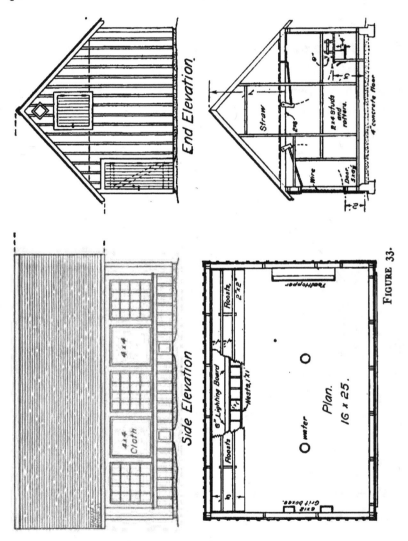

FIGURE 33.

8′ long over all. Then draw in the roof boards, vertical
siding, and door. The door is made of two thicknesses of
inch lumber, one thickness being nailed on crosswise to the

other, the outside layer being vertical. The door swings both ways on $\frac{3}{8}''$ rods as shown. Having drawn the end view, lead in the side view, getting the heights of the various lines by transferring horizontally across from the end view.

EXERCISE 9. — Draw plans of a poultry house 16' × 25', showing plan, sectional view, and end and side elevations as in Fig. 33. Use the scale $\frac{3}{8}'' = 1'$, and make the drawings on paper 18" × 24". Use a border line 15" × 22", and trim the paper to within $\frac{5}{8}''$ of the border. The pitch of the roof is $\frac{7}{16}$, the rafters being given a 7' rise, instead of the half pitch, in order that 12' material may be used for the rafters and still give room for the straw loft. The plan and sectional elevation show the standard layout for nests and roosts for a fresh-air house for 100 hens. Figure 33 may also be followed in planning a house for a smaller number of birds.

EXERCISE 10. — Draw stable plan, side and end elevations of a gambrel roof barn, the scale $\frac{1}{8}''$, $\frac{3}{16}''$, or $\frac{1}{4}''$ to the foot, depending on the size of the barn. Use a sheet of drawing paper 18" × 24". If possible, use a border line, the size depending on the amount of space the views take.

Figure 34 will give suggestions as to the proper method of proceeding. First, draw the end elevation, showing the framing of the barn. This is the basis for starting the drawings as well as for the carpenter work. Next finish the left half of the end elevation, showing siding, cornice, corner boards, etc.. Then draw the side elevation, transferring the various heights across from the end elevation. The plan of the barn should, of course, be worked out

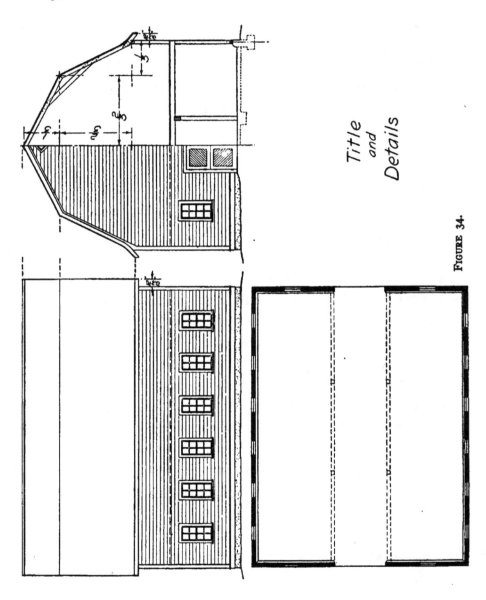

Title
and
Details

FIGURE 34.

in detail before the elevations are drawn. The plan is directly below the side elevation. The space below the end elevation can be used for the title, and, if so desired, for details of stalls, ventilation systems, etc. The end elevation gives the proper proportions for laying out the rafters of the gambrel roof. In barns up to 40' or more in width the height of the building is commonly made about equal to the width. In wider barns the height will not equal the width.

EXERCISE 11.[1] — Draw the basement and first and second floor plans of a modern house, together with a front elevation of the same. Use two sheets of paper 18″ × 24″. Draw the first and second floor plans on one sheet and the basement plan and front elevation on the other. Use the scale $\frac{1}{4}″ = 1'$. Ink the walls in solid black except for windows and doors. Put the title at the top of each sheet. The following is a list of items to be kept in mind when laying out a convenient basement, though in many cases all are not necessary.

Stairs,	Outside entrance,
Furnace,	Cistern,
Chimney,	Pneumatic tank,
Soot box in base of chimney,	Pumping apparatus,
Coal bins,	Laundry,
Coal chute,	Drying clothes (in winter),
Wood storage,	Vegetable storage,
Lighting equipment	Fruit storage.
(gas or electric lights),	

[1] Should the course in drawing not allow enough time for complete plans of a house, the first and second floor plans and basement plan might be worked out to a smaller scale on one sheet of paper, leaving the space in the lower right-hand corner for the title, similar to Fig. 34. Figure 35 illustrates the method of laying out the rough plans on cross-section paper.

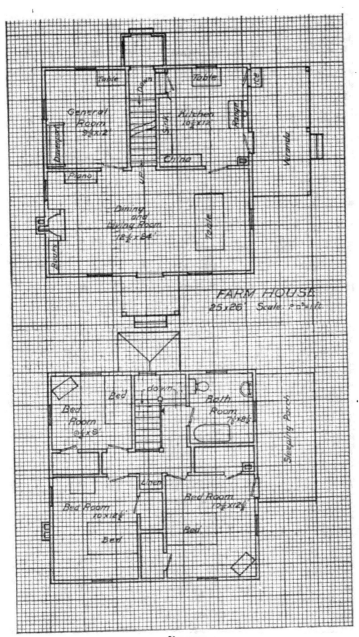

FIGURE 35.

The grading of drawings. — The three points to be considered in grading drawings, are 1, neatness; 2, lettering, figures, dimension and witness lines and arrows; 3, the actual drawings. A very good arrangement is to allow 10 points for neatness, 30 for lettering, etc., and 60 for the drawings. It is a good plan to go over all the drawings, grading them for neatness, then go over them again and grade for the lettering, etc., and finally run through the drawings the third time and grade the drawing.

СУТЬОКИИ
ПИЛАТОЬ